EXPLORING THEATER

Puppetry in Theater

George Capaccio

Cavendish Square
New York

Published in 2018 by Cavendish Square Publishing, LLC
243 5th Avenue, Suite 136, New York, NY 10016

First Edition

Cataloging-in-Publication Data

Names: Capaccio, George.
Title: Puppetry in theater / George Capaccio.
Description: New York : Cavendish Square Publishing, 2018. | Series: Exploring theater | Includes glossary and index. | Audience: Grades 7-12.
Identifiers: ISBN 9781502630056 (library bound) | ISBN 9781502634313 (pbk.) | ISBN 9781502630063 (ebook)
Subjects: LCSH: Puppets--Juvenile literature. | Puppet theater--Juvenile literature.
Classification: LCC PN1972.C36 2018 | DDC 791.5'3--dc23

Editorial Director: David McNamara
Editor: Fletcher Doyle
Copy Editor: Nathan Heidelberger
Associate Art Director: Amy Greenan
Designer: Jessica Nevins
Production Coordinator: Karol Szymczuk
Photo Research: J8 Media

The photographs in this book are used by permission and through the courtesy of: Cover The Washington Post/Getty Images; p. 4 Keith Beaty/Toronto Star/Getty Images; p. 7 Underwood Archives/Archive Photos/Getty Images; p. 9 Jeff J Mitchell/Getty Images; p. 11 Universal Pictures/Moviepix/Getty Images; p. 13 Theo Wargo/WireImage/Getty Images; p. 16 Monica Schipper/FilmMagic/Getty Images; p. 20 Luca Tettoni/Robertharding/Getty Images; p. 22 Danita Delimont/Gallo Images/Getty Images; p. 24 Anadolu Agency/Getty Images; p. 25 Scott Cornell/Shutterstock.com; p. Monica Schipper/WireImage/Getty Images; p. 31 The Asahi Shimbun/Getty Images; p. 34 Boston Globe/Getty Images; p. 39 ©iStockphoto.com/Titoslack; p. 40 George Karger/The LIFE Images Collection/Getty Images; p. 42 Krzysztof Dydynski/Lonely Planet Images/Getty Images; p. 44 Tatiana Bobkova/Shutterstock.com; p. 48 Comstock/Stockbyte/Thinkstock; p. 51 Esther Bubley/The LIFE Images Collection /Getty Images; p. 53 Frank Micelotta/Getty Images; pp. 62-63 Education Images/Universal Images Group/Getty Images; p. 64 Barcroft Media/Getty Images; p. 67 Tibor Bognar/Corbis Documentary/Getty Images; p. 69 Ullstein Bild Premium/Getty Images; p. 74 John Burke/The Image Bank/Getty Images; p. 77 Wally Skalij/Los Angeles Times/Getty Images; p. 80 Lester Cohen/WireImage/Getty Images; p. 84 The AGE/Fairfax Media/Getty Images; p. 86 ©iStockphoto.com/SolStock.

Printed in the United States of America

CONTENTS

Canadian icon Andy Barrie manipulates his marionette with a control board.

CHAPTER ONE

More Than Pulling Strings

When you think of puppets and puppet theater, what's the first thing that comes to mind? Some people might recall the Muppets, that legendary cast of characters created by **puppeteer** Jim Henson and featured on *Sesame Street*, the long-running children's (and adult!) TV show that first aired on November 10, 1969. Big Bird, Elmo, Cookie Monster, Count von Count, Bert and Ernie, and Kermit the Frog are just a few of the puppet characters Henson created to both entertain and educate generations of children.

Henson came up with the name Muppets for his creations by combining the words "puppet" and "**marionette**," a French word that goes back to the 1600s and literally means "little Mary" in reference to the Virgin Mary, the mother of Jesus. Marionettes are often made of wood and have jointed arms and legs to which strings are attached. A puppeteer, usually out of sight and overhead, moves the marionette by manipulating a **control board**. Puppet representations of Mary were among the first marionettes to appear in religious plays during the Middle Ages in Europe.

Older folks, when they think of puppets, are likely to look back to their childhood during the 1950s, before the advent of *Sesame Street* and the Muppets. As a child of the 1950s, I couldn't wait to get home from school and catch the latest episode of my favorite TV program—*The Howdy Doody Show.* The show's host, Buffalo Bob, kept kids like me glued to the TV set with the antics of his sidekick, Howdy Doody, a stringed puppet—or marionette—with a shock of red hair, a fixed smile, forty-eight freckles on his face (one for each state of the Union back then), and the look and charm of a happy-go-lucky little cowboy.

"Say, kids, what time is it?" Buffalo Bob asked the children in the Peanut Gallery (the TV studio audience) at the beginning of each show. "It's Howdy Doody time!" they roared in response. I roared right along with the kids in the Peanut Gallery, and I bet millions of kids like me, sitting in front of their black-and-white TVs, did exactly the same. That's how much we loved this show and the puppets that held us spellbound.

Howdy's puppet pals in the fictitious town of Doodyville were also marionettes, each with a distinctive voice and character, like Phineas T. Bluster, the town's mayor, Flub-a-Dub, an impossible combination of eight different animals, and Howdy's sister, Heidi Doody. Thanks to Buffalo Bob's affection for the inhabitants of Doodyville and his way of relating to them as if they were real people, we had no trouble believing they were real too and that Howdy Doody was a kid just like us.

Buffalo Bob Smith and his puppet made *The Howdy Doody Show* a popular children's TV program.

Buffalo Bob was *not* a **ventriloquist** who could carry on a believable conversation between himself and Howdy Doody or with any of the other puppets on the show. Instead, before each show, he recorded Howdy's lines, and during the show, an engineer played the recording when it was Howdy's turn to speak. Buffalo Bob also relied on highly skilled puppeteers to **animate** the marionettes in Doodyville, while offstage actors provided their unique voices. Together, these talented individuals, working as a team, demonstrated many of the skills anyone working in puppetry needs to know and master.

It's Alive!

One of the most essential skills is the ability to create the illusion of life. A successful puppet show will convince the audience—whether young or old or in between—that the **constructed actors** onstage are moving of their own free will.

But how does this happen? How do puppeteers make lifeless approximations of human and nonhuman characters come convincingly alive? "Puppets always have to try to be alive," says Adrian Kohler of the Handspring Puppet Company, which incorporates both human and constructed actors in its astonishing productions. In 2007, the members of this groundbreaking **ensemble** adapted a children's novel for the London stage. The novel, *War Horse*, was written by British author Michael Morpurgo. Albert, a young man in Devon, England, forms a deep attachment with an exceptional horse he names Joey. When Joey is sent to the battlefields of Europe during the First World War to serve in the British cavalry, Albert sets off on a perilous journey to find Joey and bring him back home.

Joey and the Dinosaurs

The Handspring Puppet Company transformed the story into a magical theatrical experience in which

Three handlers rehearse with Joey, the puppet in *War Horse,* at a military barracks.

life-size horses made of fabric-covered cane frames come to life. The show's creators made no attempt to conceal the presence of the handlers—the puppeteers responsible for **articulating** the movements of the horses. With uncanny precision and **verisimilitude**, they show Joey and the other puppet horses breathing, galloping, twitching their ears, swishing their tails, and moving with all the grace and beauty of living animals.

Three puppeteers, visible to the audience, work together to create each horse's movements. One puppeteer, standing outside the body of the horse, manipulates the head, ears, and neck; the other two, situated under the horse, move the front and rear legs. (Visit https://www.youtube.com/watch?v=dlnbIhk9jt8 for a look at how the horse works.) A theater critic who saw the Broadway production had this to say about the show:

> *Lifelike without any attempt to conceal the artifice, the creatures are magnificent, a thrilling synthesis of art and imagination. It wasn't until after heading home that I stopped to think that I had just cried over a horse that was actually made up of several props held together by visible handlers. This is the power and magic of great theater.*

Contrary to what many people regard as an art form mainly suitable for children, puppetry can appeal to all ages. It is only limited by the intelligence and imagination of the puppeteers. The origins of puppetry go back to the very beginning of human culture thousands of years ago. Throughout its long history, it has continued to adapt to ever-changing artistic styles and cultural norms, and to evolve right along with other art forms, like dance, live-actor theater, music, and sculpture. In today's world, theater audiences are witnessing a revitalization of puppetry in which constructed actors and live actors will often appear together on the stage.

Advances in technology have expanded the world of puppets beyond traditional hand-crafted dolls with moveable heads and limbs. A puppet can be just about any inanimate object given the illusion of life.

The dinosaurs in the Jurassic Park movies were brought to life through a mix of puppetry and CGI.

Think of all those movies in which puppet characters play a leading role and seem to exist as independent creations. In *Jurassic Park*, for example, most of the dinosaurs are a kind of mechanical puppet. There are no strings attached to these creatures, although there were handlers guiding many of them by remote control. In some cases, an actor inside a full-body dinosaur suit animated the animal. Nevertheless, the dinosaurs seem entirely believable, thanks to technology—namely, **animatronics** and computer-generated imagery (CGI). *Jurassic Park*, released in 1993, was the first movie to use life-size robotic dinosaurs, i.e., puppets, in which the special effects were digital.

The Nuts and Bolts of Puppetry

Beginning puppeteers are advised to experiment with simple puppets either purchased or made by hand,

and to stage performances for family and friends as a way to develop the necessary skills. An academic degree is not required to practice the art of puppetry, though some aspiring puppeteers may find it useful to major in theater in college. A solid background in the performing arts will help you develop some of the skills you'll need for working with puppets. With a bit of research, you might find a theater program that offers courses in puppetry. Your local library or community arts center may even hold puppetry workshops where you can gain some hands-on experience with puppets.

Besides the core skill of making lifeless objects appear to be alive, puppeteers have to be able to give their puppets distinct characters and to create unique voices for each puppet. Did you ever listen to the Muppets Bert and Ernie having a conversation on *Sesame Street*? You can always tell which character is speaking since their voices are so distinctive (and performed by different voice artists). Expressing character through voice and movement is a basic performance skill. And part of being a performer is understanding how a dramatic script is composed of scenes, each with its own purpose, tone, and emotional elements.

Puppeteers also have to learn the technical skills involved in controlling their puppets' movements. Of course, these will vary depending on the types of puppets you're using. The most common types are hand or glove/mitten puppets, marionettes (string puppets), **rod puppets**, and shadow puppets. Hand puppets are really part of a much larger category in

Can you spot the puppeteers operating the various animals in this scene from the stage version of *The Lion King*?

which the puppet is worn on part of the performer's body or over his or her entire body. The hand is probably the most commonly used body part because of how expressive and agile it can be. However, puppeteers also use their elbows, forearms, feet, and heads. There are even single-finger and two-finger puppets. Jim Henson's Muppets are a type of puppet known as **mitten heads**. A puppeteer working with mitten head puppets uses his or her thumb to manipulate the character's lower jaw, while the other four fingers control the expressions of the face.

There are also full-body puppets that completely cover the puppeteer's body. These are not the same as costumes since these puppets have their own bodies and physical attributes. Have you ever seen the stage version of *The Lion King*? The show's designer and director, Julie Taymor, along with her team, created more than two hundred puppets, including rod, shadow, and full-size puppets. The giraffes and elephant in the show are full-size and full-body puppets. To move the giraffes onstage, two actors have to climb 6-foot (1.8-meter) ladders to get inside the puppets and then mount pairs of stilts. "Bertha," the 13-foot- (4 m) long by 9-foot- (2.7 m) wide elephant puppet, needs four actors to create her movements.

For the most common types of puppets, there are some very basic skills you need to get under your belt: lip **synchronization**, proper mouth movements, eye contact, correct posture and height, lifelike movements, and proper entrances and exits. Let's take a closer look at each of these skills.

Lip Synchronization

How do you make your puppet look like she's really speaking (when in reality her voice is coming from you or a recording)? The trick is to open and close her mouth in sync with the syllables that make up each word. Open her mouth at the beginning of each syllable and close it at the end. Mastering this skill takes lots of practice, especially since beginners tend to close the puppet's mouth when it should be opening. If a spoken word has three syllables, then you should open your puppet's mouth three times. And you don't need to open it all the way. Those big, wide-open mouths work best when your puppet is shouting or expressing a strong feeling, like anger.

Proper Mouth Movement

Take a few moments to stand in front of a mirror and watch yourself talking out loud. You'll notice that when you speak, your jaw moves up and down—not your entire head. The same holds true for your puppet. When she speaks, her lower jaw should also move up and down, and not her head. When you first begin practicing this movement, you may notice how much easier it is to raise the puppet's head instead of lowering the jaw. To overcome this tendency, when using a hand puppet, try moving your thumb downward without moving your fingers up. Tricky, huh?

Eye Contact

When you and a friend are having a conversation, do you face each other and maintain eye contact, or do you tend to look away and avoid eye contact? If your friend is looking everywhere else but in your direction, how does that make you feel? Left out? Ignored? Lack of eye contact may be all too frequent in real life, but in puppet theater, it's a major no-no. If two puppets are having a conversation, they should look at each other as they speak. And the same is true if the conversation is between a puppet and the puppeteer. The only time puppets should look directly at the audience is when they are actually addressing

Ventriloquist Paul Zerdin maintains eye contact with the puppet he's talking to. Zerdin was the winner of *America's Got Talent* in 2015.

the audience. Otherwise, they should maintain eye contact with another puppet character or with the puppeteer. If your puppet is performing a specific action like turning the pages of a book, then make sure she is focused on the action and not looking somewhere else.

Correct Posture and Height

When you walk on a flat surface, like a sidewalk, you don't sink into the pavement or bob up and down like a cork in the ocean. Nor do you sway from side to side. Instead, you keep to a steady course while maintaining an upright position and a consistent height. Inexperienced puppeteers, however, may not have the same degree of control of their puppets as they do of themselves. To make your puppets appear lifelike, you need to practice moving them as if they have legs of their own and are standing on a flat, hard surface.

So how do you achieve this effect? With hand puppets, the trick is to keep your arm at a right angle to the floor of the stage and your hand at the same height. At first, your arm may soon grow tired from the effort of holding it upright. But with practice, you'll develop the necessary strength to see you through an entire performance.

Speaking of arms, most people have a dominant arm and a weaker arm. In puppetry, it helps enormously to develop both arms instead of always relying on the dominant one. During a lengthy performance, you can rest one arm while using the other, thus conserving your energy. And think of how much easier it will be to operate two puppets at the same time if both your arms are equally strong.

Lifelike Movements

Your puppet's movements must correspond to what she is thinking and feeling and be consistent with her character—the type of person (or creature) she is. Random, unfocused movements just don't work. Like a live actor in a play, your puppet should move with purpose and avoid any actions or gestures that have nothing to do with the role she is performing. In many puppet plays, once the puppets are onstage, their movements tend to be limited. But even when they are relatively stationary, they still need to appear to be listening, observing, and responding to whatever is going on in the moment. They can remain in place but must seem fully alive.

And here's another tip for making your puppets appear lifelike: Connect their arm and hand gestures with what they are saying and the feelings behind the words, just the way we do when we communicate with one another. Similarly, make the most of your puppets' ability to move their heads. For example, a slight tilt to one side will convey a look of curiosity, while a droopy, downward movement will express disappointment or sadness.

Proper Entrances and Exits

You might think that bringing your puppet onstage at the beginning of a performance or having her leave when the show is over is easy as pie. It's not. While there are many ways of handling entrances and exits, they all have one thing in common: They maintain the illusion that the puppet has legs and can walk all by herself.

So how do you create this illusion? Simple. Imagine there is a staircase with three to four stairs that your puppet is ascending to the puppet stage when she enters or descending when she exits. Practice bobbing the head of your puppet up and down to simulate the movement of someone walking on a flat surface. When it's time for your puppet to make an entrance, have her ascend the imaginary steps in a series of distinct movements. With each step, move your puppet up and then have her come down slightly. As a puppeteer, you can achieve the same effect by having your puppet bend backward and then straighten her body with each step.

Reverse the process for descending, but have the puppet turn and look down to find the first step before descending. Hint: When figuring out the correct height of your puppet onstage, remember that if the puppet is too low, she may look like she's sinking in quicksand. If she's too high, the audience might see your arm.

Just a reminder: The skills we've discussed so far are the ones you'll want to become familiar with when you start working with puppets. They are especially applicable to marionettes, rod puppets, and puppets worn by the puppeteer, such as hand puppets. But the world of puppetry, as we've seen, also includes computer-animated puppets, like the dinosaurs in *Jurassic Park*, and even two-dimensional, or flat, puppets, such as shadow puppets and those made from reflected light!

These puppeteers are working as a team to bring their rod puppets to life in this show from India.

CHAPTER TWO

Go, Team, Go!

Puppets not only come in a variety of shapes and sizes, they also use different animation methods or systems, and these in turn can be combined to create hybrid forms of animation. The simplest and most common method for making a puppet seem lifelike is for the puppeteer to wear the puppet on part of his or her body. Moving a hand or foot, for example, automatically animates the puppet.

Puppeteers on *Sesame Street* gave life to the Muppets by using a technique that blended hand (or mitten) puppetry with rod puppetry. Rods provide external forms of manipulation. Rod puppets can vary in size from tiny figures to giant dragons or other larger-than-life creatures requiring multiple operators.

The rods are made of wood, wire, or some other sturdy substance, and are attached above, below, or behind the puppet. The number of puppet parts that need to be manipulated will determine the number of rods that are used. As you might have guessed, rod puppets can be quite expressive, capable of large, dramatic movements as well as much more subtle ones.

The oldest technique for manipulating puppets involves the use of string or cord. Have you ever seen or played with a **pantin**? That's a French word referring to the cutout of a human character with a jointed body and limbs. To make the arms and legs suddenly fly up, all you have to do is pull the cord attached to the bottom of the figure.

The use of string or cord gets much more complicated, however. Marionettes are string puppets. They might use only one or two strings, or many more. Marionette puppets in Myanmar use as many as two dozen strings attached to many different parts of the puppet's body. This allows the puppeteer to **execute** very intricate movements, like having the puppet perform complex acrobatics.

Marionette puppets in Myanmar, formerly known as Burma, are capable of very complex movements.

Whatever the number of strings, they have to be attached to something the puppeteer can hold and control. Typically, the control board is a wooden cross. The puppeteer can move all the strings at the same time or select one string at a time. For more complex manipulations, the puppeteer might employ two controls—one for the body as a whole and the other for specific parts.

I like to imagine that our ancient Paleolithic ancestors spent many a firelit evening entertaining themselves and their children by using their hands to cast shadows on the walls of a cave or other habitation. Who knows, they might even have accompanied their shadow play with a bit of narration: "The saber-toothed tiger got ready to pounce on the wooly mammoth, when all of a sudden …"

We still get a kick out of using our hands to create shadow puppets. Of course, things other than hands can be used to create shadow puppets. You can use two-dimensional puppets created from paper, wood, plastic, metal, or whatever, either solid or carved into intricate patterns. Another variable is how much light can pass through them. Opaque shadow puppets create black images on a screen or other surface; translucent shadow puppets, on the other hand, can transmit color.

How does the puppeteer make the shadow puppets move? Simple. He or she attaches the puppet to some type of rod, which could be anything from a chopstick to a skewer for grilled vegetables. When the puppet is placed between a source of light and a screen, the puppet's image or shadow will appear on the screen.

Syrian refugee children enjoy a shadow puppet show with translucent puppets that can transmit color.

If the puppeteer wants a sharp, well-defined image, he or she needs to hold the puppet close to the screen. By positioning it farther away, he or she can make the image appear more spread out, with less definition.

Beyond Strings, Rods, and Hands

Some really innovative, experimental artists are going back to the basics of fire, water, and air to manipulate their puppets. In Russia, the Moscow Shadow Theater staged a puppet performance of *Swan Lake*, a famous ballet by the Russian composer Tchaikovsky. One of the female puppet characters is transformed into a swan by burning away her paper exterior, revealing the foil-covered swan beneath. Other artists have experimented with puppets made of ice. Audiences

Dozens of handlers keep this helium-filled Paddington Bear from floating off into space.

expect to see puppets perform some kind of action. These ice puppets are limited to one, and only one, action—melting!

The use of air to manipulate puppets is actually not very big news in the world of theater. Macy's department store has been doing this since 1924, when it held its first Thanksgiving Day Parade in New York City. Now, many decades later, the tradition is still going strong. Giant helium-filled balloon puppets are one of its most popular attractions. The balloon characters, anchored by ropes, are a kind of marionette. But instead of dangling from strings, they float above the heads of their handlers, in the streets of Manhattan. The supersize balloons have changed over the years to reflect the changing times. Nowadays, you can see inflated versions of SpongeBob SquarePants, Angry Birds' Red, and other iconic personalities from popular culture.

Each of these balloon puppets is operated by a highly organized team of between fifty and one hundred people. The job of holding the ropes attached to the balloons is anything but easy. In fact, you can't become a handler unless you're over eighteen, weigh at least 120 pounds (54.4 kilograms), are in excellent shape, and have no heart problems. When the balloon is in the air, it can feel like you're trying to keep a full-grown tiger from yanking you off your feet. In the early fall, balloon handlers typically attend "boot camp" to work out and prepare for the job.

Avenue Q: Mixing It Up

The importance of teamwork in puppet theater is clearly evident in the staging of *Avenue Q*. The show centers on Princeton, a twenty-something college graduate who majored in English and is now struggling to turn his dreams into reality. He finds a shabby apartment on Avenue Q, a fictitious street in a multicultural New York neighborhood where the neighbors in his building soon become an important

Avenue Q's Ben Durocher, Kerri Brackin, and Jason Jacoby perform outside in New York.

night's performance, was the responsibility of one person—Kristine Hummel. She had to make sure each of the puppets' eyeballs was scratch-free. She also had to repair any broken rods that were used to manipulate the puppets and mend any socks worn as hand puppets. After a performance, she stored the puppets inside crates with their own hair dryers, since moisture from the actors' sweaty palms could damage the puppets.

Shakespeare's *The Tempest* and Japanese Bunraku

Let's jump back in time from *Avenue Q* in the twenty-first century to a magical island in the very distant past. The island is inhabited by spirits, including Ariel, the dutiful servant of a master magician named Prospero. In the early 1600s, William Shakespeare wrote *The Tempest*, a play about Prospero and Ariel and the other characters on the island. The play focuses on Prospero's attempt to regain his position as the Duke of Milan after his brother, Antonio, forced him to leave his home behind.

On the island where he and his daughter end up, Prospero behaves very much like a master puppeteer. With his power over magical forces, he is able to control most of the humans and spirits who inhabit his island kingdom.

In our own time, Christopher Parks, a former director of education for the McCarter Theater Center for the Performing Arts in New Jersey, adapted *The Tempest* for middle and high school audiences.

Two additional puppeteers, dressed all in black, blend into the background of this Bunraku performance in Japan.

Although the forty-five-minute adaptation employs different forms of puppetry, most of the puppets are life-size figures manipulated by human performers. As with the *Avenue Q* play, *The Tempest, a Puppet Play* depends on teamwork, especially in the way the puppets are handled during the performance. Parks, who also directed the show, wanted the puppets to come as close as possible to living, breathing human beings. To this end, he incorporated the stylized movement techniques from **Bunraku**, an ancient form of Japanese theater that continues to draw audiences.

In Bunraku productions, three highly trained puppeteers handle the puppets representing the play's major characters. The puppets are about half the size of an ordinary person and wear costumes appropriate to the medieval era of Japan's long history. Bringing these puppets to life requires an extraordinary degree of teamwork. The chief puppeteer manipulates the puppet's head and right hand. One of his partners controls the puppet's left hand; the third person operates the legs. During performances, the puppeteers are dressed entirely in black. Even their heads are covered. They have to learn how to coordinate their movements so perfectly, so seamlessly, that audiences soon forget they are watching puppets and instead fall under the spell of master puppeteers creating the illusion of life.

Teamwork in Bunraku extends beyond the harmonious interplay of the puppeteers. This form of theater also incorporates the talents of narrators and musicians. They work closely together to enhance and deepen the emotional atmosphere of Bunraku drama. The musicians play the samisen, a three-stringed instrument originally introduced by the Chinese. The narrators tell the story, provide the voices of each character, and sing during the sung portions of the text. Like the puppeteers, narrators undergo decades of practice before they master their art. Only master narrators are permitted to slightly alter the narration.

In the McCarter production of *The Tempest, a Puppet Play*, Christopher Parks, the director, assigned two puppeteers—not three—to each major puppet character. Like the puppeteers in Bunraku, they had to learn how to coordinate their movements and work together as a tightly knit team. The lead puppeteer in *The Tempest* was responsible for manipulating the puppet's mouth, eyes, and left arm, and for providing the character's voice. His partner controlled the right arm by moving a rod attached to the puppet's wrist, while holding its body with his left hand. He was also responsible for orchestrating all of the puppet's large movements. To accomplish this feat, he strapped the puppet's feet to his own; when the puppeteer moved, so did the puppet's legs. Again borrowing from the Bunraku tradition, *The Tempest* puppeteers were dressed in black, which allowed them to practically disappear from view during the performances.

The Bread and Puppet Theater located in Vermont started in 1963. Its performances are always a stunning combination of music, dance, slapstick comedy, and hard-hitting political satire. Its latest creation—*Faust 3*—looks at working class life in America and incorporates finger puppets, hand puppets, masks, and one puppet that's too big for some **venues**. Fourteen performers are in the show. There are so many roles, the actors have to play multiple parts. In order to make each performance remarkable, a key ingredient must be present—teamwork.

As these examples from the world of theater illustrate, puppetry encompasses a wide range of styles and puppet types, from simple sock puppets to gigantic balloons, from mere shadows on a wall to full-size, three-dimensional figures. Puppetry is also about people working together as a team. Each team member has his or her own skills and talents to contribute and his or her own unique vision or perspective about what will make a compelling puppet play. Set designers, musicians, and of course puppeteers are some of the key players in puppet theater, whether intended for an audience of children or grown-ups.

In this adaptation of Hans Christian Andersen's "The Snow Queen," the Queen is a giant puppet.

CHAPTER THREE

Three Stages of Production

Putting on a puppet play requires a whole lot of teamwork—unless of course it's a one-person show, with one puppeteer handling one or more puppets. If puppetry is a form of theater that interests you, you'll want to have a solid understanding of what goes into creating a puppet performance. For starters, as a theatrical form, puppetry shares many characteristics with live- actor theater. Puppeteers need to develop acting skills. They have to be able to bring their characters to life, **project** their voices, and tap into the emotional ingredients of each scene. Like other kinds of performers, puppeteers may have to improvise occasionally, especially when the unexpected happens, like forgetting your lines or missing your entrance cue, or when a prop is misplaced or fails to function properly, or one of the puppets is missing. Since many theater companies make no attempt to conceal or disguise the puppet handlers, puppeteers also need to be comfortable onstage in front of an audience, instead of hidden behind a puppet stage curtain.

a mystery? Each of these different forms, or genres, will influence the way the plot, the characters, and the themes develop.

Similarly, by changing the setting or locale of a story, you'll discover new ways to present your main idea. Suppose the two leading characters in your play are mythical creatures like a unicorn and Bigfoot (the mysterious wild man of the Pacific Northwest forests). In your play-in-progress, additional puppet characters might be a couple of backpackers in the wilderness. What kinds of changes can you imagine if instead of a wilderness setting in the present, the story takes place on a distant planet in the future, or in a completely made-up environment?

The process of developing a play, including a puppet play, is a very creative process. Whether your starting point is a theme, a conflict, a particular location, or some other story element, at some point you will need to write down the results of your improvisations and continue to refine the writing until you've got yourself an honest-to-goodness script ready for the next stage of production—rehearsals.

Whether you're creating a script from scratch or adapting a story (authored or traditional), keep in mind that the play's characters are meant to be puppets. If you already have a bunch of puppets on hand, they might be all you need to get your playwriting off to a great start. Their appearances and how they look in different groupings can inspire all sorts of ideas. So have fun.

When you and your fellow puppeteers get together for a brainstorming session, bring out the puppets. Handle them. Play with them. Let them

Take stock of the puppets you have when writing a play to perform. The puppets can serve as inspiration to the playwrights.

spark your creativity and suggest ideas that could be the seeds of an original puppet play. And while you're brainstorming and improvising, add some music to the mix. Music is another terrific idea booster. It can suggest characters, create atmosphere, and even conjure up entire scenarios.

A Delicate Balance

Plays from live-actor theater are one more valuable source of material for your own work. In 2013, Eric Bass, the co–artistic director of Vermont's Sandglass Theater, went to Germany to work with a famous puppet theater. The company wanted Bass to direct a play. After some research, he chose *The Glass*

Menagerie by the American playwright Tennessee Williams. His reading of the play convinced him that an adaptation with puppets would be an exciting new direction for this staple of the American theater. The play concerns a struggling family in St. Louis in the 1940s. At the heart of the play is Laura Wingfield, a shy young woman who hardly ever leaves her family's house. Her collection of miniature glass animals is her dearest possession. They have their own world, and in that world, Laura feels completely at home.

In the original Broadway production of *The Glass Menagerie*, the actress playing Laura holds up a figurine from her collection.

For the German theater's production of this play, Bass envisioned combining human actors with puppet representations of the main characters. During the performance, the actors interacted with each other and with puppet characters. For instance, Laura's brother, Tom, interacts with the puppet version of their mother, Amanda. At other times, the human actors playing Tom and Amanda interact with each other, and so on.

The character of Laura is played by two puppets. One is a marionette; the other is made of glass-like resin. Laura's puppet self can easily enter the world of her glass animals, who share her delicate, transparent nature.

Assessing the Script

As you develop your own script, you'll want to step back from time to time to ask yourself if the script would be best served entirely by puppets or by a combination of human actors and puppets. In fact, you might even create a checklist of things to keep in mind as you head into rehearsals. Here's a sample checklist for a children's puppet play:

- Is the material appropriate for the intended age of your audience?
- Is the language easy enough for children to understand?
- Will they be able to follow the action?
- Can you make the necessary scene changes smoothly and quickly without slowing down the action?

The stars of this outdoor puppet performance are Michael Jackson and Elvis Presley.

- If props are included, will the puppets be able to handle them?
- Do you have a compelling blend of action, dialogue, and scene changes that will focus and hold the attention of your audience?
- Will music and/or sound effects enhance the story or get in its way?

As a general rule of thumb, very young audiences are more likely to remain attentive when the play is no longer than fifteen to twenty minutes. Children ages ten and above should be able to stay with a play that is between thirty-five and forty-five minutes in length but not much longer.

Some people with experience in puppet theater endorse the use of scrolled scripts, so the actors are never in any danger of forgetting their lines or missing their cues. One script, slowly unrolling in the course of the play, is especially useful for beginners who may not be comfortable with memorization. Of course, this technique is best performed out of sight. Only the puppets should be visible during performances in which actors are relying on reading a script, rolled or otherwise.

The Next Step: Rehearsals

OK, you've got your script and are ready to go. What's next? Rehearsals. Assuming you're part of a cast of puppeteers working on a play, you will likely need the services of a director—someone with an objective perspective to guide and shape the play and the performances. Every director, whether working in puppet theater or live-actor theater, will have his or her own style, unique sense of the best way to proceed, and vision of what the final product should look like. Even if you're a solo performer planning a one-person puppet show, the quality of your work will benefit if you bring in someone to observe your rehearsals and initial performances, and provide supportive feedback about what does or doesn't work.

Shadow Play

Let's look more closely at one-person puppet shows. That might be just the format to get you started on the road to becoming a skilled puppeteer. How about

In this wonderful example of shadow puppet theater, a little prince confronts a dragon.

doing your own show with shadow puppets? This traditional form of puppetry goes all the way back to ancient China. Here are the things you need for a one-person shadow puppet show:

- A simple story, lasting five to ten minutes and suitable for small children.
- Black cardstock for the characters in your story and any props or scenery.
- Scissors.

- Wooden sticks or skewers.
- Black tape or glue for attaching the sticks to the figures.
- A large piece of cardboard or foam core.
- Light source.
- White cloth or paper for a screen.
- Sound makers (optional).

Imagine that your local library is planning a festival featuring Aesop's fables, and you've been invited to present one of these classic stories. After some thought, you decide to perform "The Tortoise and the Hare" as a shadow puppet play. In this short tale, the two animals race through the woods to see which one is faster. Hare is much too sure of himself and figures he has plenty of time to grab a snack and take a nap. As a result, he loses the race, and Tortoise, first to cross the finish line, delivers that crushing moral: "Slow and steady wins the race."

Now that you've got your story, you need to create shapes for the characters, props, and set pieces. You can draw them yourself or search for them in books or online. Once you have the shapes, lay them on your heavy black paper and cut them out to make silhouettes. Glue or tape the sticks to the back of each cutout figure and prepare your stage.

Your stage can be nothing more complicated than a white cloth suspended across a door frame. Your audience will sit on one side of the cloth, and you'll sit on the other with your puppets and whatever you might need for creating sound effects. Make sure you've got a source of light and an electrical outlet on your side. And don't forget to set up that large piece of cardboard or foam core along the bottom of the cloth to keep you well hidden and to create a dark space in which to work your magic.

Now, switch on the light and practice, practice, practice manipulating the puppets in front of the light. Their shadows will appear on the screen. You'll probably need to experiment with the light to get the shadows just the way you want them. Finally, try telling the story as you handle the puppets. Use different voices for the different animal characters. You might enlist a friend or family member to make the sound effects. Once you're able to smoothly tell the story while manipulating the puppets and their shadows, you're ready to put on a show for real!

Getting Ready to Rehearse

In the case of a puppet play involving more than one performer and more challenging types of puppets, some training may be necessary before the rehearsals if the performers have little or no experience handling puppets. The main purpose of this training is to introduce them to puppetry and to the challenges they'll need to overcome once they begin working with the puppets. Hand puppets are an excellent choice for beginning puppeteers. Marionettes, however, require considerably more training. Puppeteers need to learn not only how to animate them but how to cross in front of other actors without the strings of the puppets becoming entangled.

During the pre-rehearsal training, the director may use theater games and exercises in which the actors work together to solve problems, develop confidence in their own abilities, and begin to cultivate a team spirit. Ideally, this work will transform a group of performers into a motivated, highly functioning ensemble capable of delivering a quality performance each and every time. Before formal rehearsals begin, the initial training period can be done without puppets. For newcomers to puppet theater, the introduction of puppets at this early stage of the learning process may be too inhibiting. On the other hand, training sessions that are fun and low-stress will free up creative energy and prepare the cast for the work to come. They will also give the director an opportunity to identify the strengths of the players, and this in turn will enable him or her to make casting decisions based on these strengths.

Rehearsals for Real

Pre-training is over. The director has decided which actors will play which roles. Let's assume he or she has chosen to use a previously published script instead of one that evolved from group improvisations. In any case, it's time for the cast to come together and do a first reading of the play. What happens during the rehearsal process in puppet theater is not significantly different from the way actors rehearse in live-actor theater. The rehearsal space should approximate the

These three young actors are going over their lines backstage prior to a first reading and rehearsals with their puppets.

dimensions of the performance space, so actors know from the get-go how much room they have in which to move and gesture.

During a first reading, the director typically discusses his or her interpretation of the play and how he or she sees the various characters. For puppet plays, the director may also go over manipulation techniques for the puppets. Some of the puppets may pose special problems that the actors will need to overcome. A wise course of action is to allow the actors to handle the puppets on their own without having to practice specific ways of moving them. Through experimentation, the actors are more likely to discover problems, as well as solutions to those problems. And this, in turn, will go a long way toward getting the actors to "own" the puppets and take greater responsibility for the quality of their work.

In subsequent rehearsals, the director will start **blocking** the action. For live-actor theater, this entails laying out the movement patterns for the entire show. For example, when does character A cross from upstage right to downstage left? How far does character B walk before he turns around and exits? Where are the entrances and exits? When blocking a puppet play, the director needs to determine how much stage space each puppet will occupy and then block the movement in relation to this space and the effects of the puppet's movements on its handler, who may be offstage or onstage, depending on the nature of the production.

At this point in the rehearsal process, no attempt is made to conceal the puppeteers. The director needs to observe the overall flow of action between the onstage and offstage areas, and to identify any potential "traffic" problems. For instance, during a blocking session, the director may notice that two of the actors are always getting in each other's way when they attempt to change puppets. It's up to the director to solve this problem or have the actors come up with a practical solution.

Puppet Stages

The type of stage will determine how the action is blocked. Traditional hand-puppet stages, also known as "Punch and Judy" stages, are lightweight booths large enough for one puppeteer to stand inside and operate one or more puppets. The small size of these "puppet booths" limits the amount of action that is possible and the number of puppets that can be used. And since there is only one puppeteer, there's little need for extensive blocking.

There is no "one size fits all" puppet stage. The size of the stage depends on the nature of the production, the types of puppets, and the needs of the puppeteers. A ventriloquist doesn't even need a stage. Ventriloquists are skillful entertainers who can make their voices appear to be coming from the puppet of an animal or a person. Way back in the early days of television, the American ventriloquist Shari Lewis charmed children with her sock puppet character Lamb Chop. Lewis and her puppet characters have had several of their own TV shows, including *The Shari Lewis Show*, which made its debut in 1960.

Fast-forward sixty years and meet Jeff Dunham, one of today's most popular ventriloquists, who is also a stand-up comedian. Six of his TV specials can be viewed on the Comedy Central channel. As a ventriloquist, Dunham has created a wild array of puppets with which he performs. His puppet characters include José Jalapeño on a Stick, Amazing Ken, Little Jeff, Sweet Daddy Dee, and Bubba J. If Dunham's popularity as a ventriloquist is any indication, then the art of puppetry is still very much alive and well.

A small stage may be just fine for hand puppets. Marionettes, however, need larger stages since the puppeteers must stand on a weight-bearing bridge behind the performing area and lean over a railing when they manipulate their puppets. Human actors

Shari Lewis delighted young audiences with puppet characters Lamb Chop and Charlie Horse.

can easily cross in front of each other onstage. This kind of movement is not so easy, however, for performers operating marionettes on strings. Achieving smooth crosses with this type of puppet requires very careful blocking.

Some puppet plays are performed in living-actor theaters without a secondary stage for the puppets and their handlers. These productions incorporate

RICHARD HUNT, MASTER PUPPETEER

From a very young age, Richard Hunt knew he was destined to follow in his family's footsteps and work in some aspect of show business. Hunt was born in New York City in 1951. As a child, he loved watching the Muppets on TV. "I'd drop anything to watch them," he said. "I thought they were weird."

His enjoyment of shows like *The Muppet Show* inspired Hunt to try his hand at puppetry. While in middle school and high school, he entertained neighborhood children with his own puppet shows. After graduating from high school, he got a job reading weather reports at a local radio station. That job was a far cry from what he truly wanted to do with his life. According to his mother, Hunt took his first step toward making his dreams come true while watching an episode of *Sesame Street.* He phoned Henson Associates, the company responsible for producing *The Muppet Show* and the characters that appear on *Sesame Street.* Hunt asked the Henson people if they were hiring puppeteers. Much to his surprise, Jim Henson, the company's founder, and a few of his colleagues were auditioning puppeteers that very same day. They invited him to come down to the office and try out for a part.

Hunt did such a good job he was hired on the spot. Only eighteen years old, he never looked back and went on to become a beloved member of the *Sesame Street* cast of puppeteers and a main performer on *The Muppet Show.* He died in 1992.

Hugh Jackman interacts with Rod and his handler from *Avenue Q*.

life-size and even larger puppets interacting with human actors. With a much larger space, there is substantially more freedom to manipulate the puppets while exploiting all the resources of a professional theater, including high-tech lighting and sound systems. Think *The Lion King* or *War Horse* as examples of plays with human and constructed actors performing on full-scale stages with dramatic music, lighting, and sound, and beautifully designed sets and costumes.

rehearsal is also the time when the director expects cast and crew to put all the training and practice behind them and perform to the best of their abilities. The dress rehearsal is done with full costumes, props, scenery, and all the lighting and sound cues.

Often, a theater will schedule one or more **preview** performances to test audience reaction and do any final tweaking before opening night. Previews allow the creative team (artistic director, set designer, sound and lighting directors, props manager, and costume director) to note and fix any potential problems, like sound effects that are too soft or too loud, songs that don't work, or dialogue that needs to be cut.

Once the show is up and running, the director's job is over. Now it's up to the performers and the technicians to "carry the ball" by assuming responsibility for the quality of their work and all the parts that make up the production—lighting, sound, props, sets, puppets, and actors.

Let the Show Begin!

Many puppet theater companies spend a fair amount of time on the road, performing in different venues. If the company specializes in children's shows, it might find itself in a school auditorium one day, a library another day, at a fair or festival during the weekend, or at some other outdoor event where families with small children will be in attendance. Other companies, like Puppet Showplace Theater in Brookline, Massachusetts, have their own theater. Audiences come to them to see puppet shows. Besides performances on their main stage, Puppet Showplace Theater also offers touring shows for schools, libraries, and other locations. Their **repertoire** features shows for children ages two and up. As a well-established community resource, Puppet Showplace Theater has expanded its services to include workshops, evening performances for teens and adults, and youth workshops for building puppets, creating puppet plays, and performing with puppets.

Preperformance Tasks

As a member of a touring company, you would soon discover that every performance, no matter where it takes place, has a "before" and an "after." Before a performance, there are a number of logistical matters that need to be addressed. How will you get the set pieces, costumes, puppets, and any equipment to the performance venue? How many people will it take to unload the car, van, or truck and complete the setup so the show is ready to go? If you're a solo performer or part of a small theater company, it's likely that you'll be responsible for some, if not all, of these matters. In larger companies with sizeable budgets, there might be a separate crew that handles the transportation and setup of the show.

As an actor, I was once a member of a children's theater company. One of our touring shows was an adaptation of Mary Shelley's novel *Frankenstein*. The show toured colleges and universities in northern New England. The set for the show was designed as a series of ramps supported on metal scaffolding with dozens of heavy pipes, nuts and bolts, and couplings to make sure the joints were secure and the whole thing wouldn't collapse. There were four actors in the show and no production crew. Each time we arrived at a venue, we actors had to unload the set, fit the pipes together, raise the scaffolding, set up the lighting, and then get into our costumes.

The setup alone wore us out. By show time, we were exhausted, and our performances suffered as a result of our not having enough energy. To make matters worse, assembling the metal pipes was not only tiring; it was a frustrating ordeal that tested our tempers to the breaking point and on at least one occasion almost led to a fistfight between two of the actors.

The moral of this story is that there's more to performing than just showing up at the performance venue. Whether you do a one-person puppet show or are one of several puppeteers in a theater company, there are many steps you can take to make your arrival and setup comparatively easy and stress free, leaving you the time you need to prepare for the performance. For starters, be sure to communicate with the person who is sponsoring your show. This might be a librarian, school principal or teacher, member of a parent teacher organization (PTO), the organizer of a public event such as an arts and crafts fair, or the parents of a child whose birthday you're celebrating with your puppet show.

Whoever your sponsor or contact person is, send them a reminder at least one week in advance. You can do this with a card, email, text message, or phone call. Let them know what time you plan to arrive at the venue, how long the show will run, the exact start time, and any special requirements you have. These might include a certain number of electrical outlets, a room in which to change into your costume, and enough space for the puppet stage (if you're traveling with your own stage). Also tell your sponsor if you'll need someone on hand to help you unload your equipment and handle any lighting or sound cues.

Your goal is to establish a friendly relationship with the people who have invited you to perform. You want them not only to appreciate your work but to remember your visit as a positive experience they will hopefully want to repeat. By being clear and upfront about your requirements and making sure your sponsor knows exactly what to expect, you'll go a long way toward making your preperformance time a great on-ramp to the show itself.

In addition to sending out a helpful reminder, be sure to rehearse setting up for your show. You want to know beforehand how long it takes, what tools may be required, and how many people are needed to accomplish the setup in an efficient, timely manner. Can you carry the equipment by yourself, or do you need helpers? For heavy items, would it be better to use a **dolly**? Is one car big enough to handle everything you need for the show, or does it require something larger, such as a van or even a small truck?

The actual setup can serve as a physical warm-up for you and your fellow performers so that you're ready to start the show with a full tank of energy. If you're hauling around your own puppet stage, it's advisable to invest in one that is lightweight and easy to install, break down, and store.

Seeing the Big Picture

Beyond the nuts and bolts of preparing to perform, a successful puppet theater company will need to consider some larger questions and issues, and to find answers before they even hit the road and take their shows on tour:

What size audience will allow the solo performer or puppet theater company to demonstrate what they do best? Some performers are at their best in front of a small audience, while others are more at home with large audiences. It may sometimes be necessary to turn down gigs if the anticipated audience is just too big for the kind of show being offered.

What age group is the target audience? Puppet Showplace Theater, mentioned earlier in this chapter, has developed specific shows for different age groups. Wisely, it doesn't promote shows that are supposedly for all ages. While some shows may actually work for a wide range of ages, a more realistic approach is to decide beforehand whether you want to perform for children, teens, or adults, and then create shows that will appeal to your chosen audience.

In what sort of venue will the performance take place? If outdoors, will the sun be shining in the eyes of the audience, making it difficult for them to see the performers? If indoors, will the heating or cooling systems need to be adjusted in order to create an environment that is neither too hot nor too cold?

If the show takes place in a school gymnasium, the children may need to sit on mats on the floor and not on bleachers, and a sound system may be necessary to overcome the poor acoustics of school gyms.

Action!

The stage is set. The puppets are in place. The performers are ready. The audience is seated. A bit of music coming through the sound system may be just the thing to set the mood and prepare the audience for what's to come. Should you engage them in any participatory activities before the official beginning of the show? Well, that depends on the type of audience and whether interactive activities are likely to get them so riled up they won't be able to settle down and concentrate on the performance. On the other hand, preshow activities with the audience may succeed in capturing their attention for the show.

House lights dim. Stage lights come up as the preshow music fades out. The show begins. Give it all you've got. Above all, have fun. Enjoy the flow of energy between you and your fellow performers and between you and the audience. Bring the puppets to life with all the skills you've mastered through long hours of practice.

And when the show is over and the audience is applauding, you'll have already decided whether to stay out of sight and let the puppets take a bow. For young audiences, it might be better to preserve the mystery of puppet theater by remaining hidden until the children have left the performing space. It all

On a sandy beach, families enjoy a Punch and Judy puppet performance. A puppeteer inside the portable stage manipulates these two hand puppets.

depends on what sort of memory you want to leave them with. Older audiences, including adults, will likely enjoy seeing you take a bow right along with the puppets.

Before Saying Goodbye

The performance may be over, but there's still work to be done. It's time to **strike** the show. You've got to store the puppets and the props, break down the set, unplug any electrical cords, lug everything out of the venue, and load it into the car or van. Will you need assistants, or can you do it all by yourself?

Don't forget to thank your sponsor for arranging your visit. If you have information about any new shows or about your current performance schedule, let your sponsor know. Once you've finished striking the show and said your good-byes, the final stage of the performance is over. You get behind the wheel of your vehicle, roll down the window, and wave one last good-bye as you drive off, feeling the satisfaction that comes with having given a first-rate performance.

Manipulating puppets can put a strain on the body and cause fatigue. Actors may need to increase their fitness to perform.

CHAPTER FOUR

Some Perils of Puppetry

Beginning puppeteers are bound to make mistakes. Even experienced puppeteers will, from time to time, miss a cue, forget their lines, or commit a slipup, or blooper, that will leave the audience laughing hysterically and the puppeteer feeling somewhat embarrassed. However, making mistakes is part of life. We all make them, no matter how hard we've practiced doing something or how skilled we've become in a particular activity.

Some of the difficulties that puppeteers experience may result not from incompetence or lack of skill but from simple physical strain. Think about it: keeping a puppet in the proper position while making exact, meaningful gestures and movements requires strength and stamina. These qualities take time to develop. One master puppeteer said that when he was just starting out it took him two months to be able to keep his arms upright during a one-hour performance without feeling the effects of strain.

Imagine sitting behind and below a puppet stage and having to hold your hand puppet over your head for an entire show. Not easy. And if you're operating a marionette, then you've got to stand on a platform while bending over a railing with your arms outstretched and doing your best to keep your puppet's feet flat on the floor of the stage. It's an awkward position and one that is sure to put strain on your lower back and tax the muscles in your arms and shoulders.

Tired Arms = Lazy Puppets

If you're tired and your arms start to ache, there's a good chance you'll begin to make some of the mistakes puppeteers commonly make, especially when they're starting out. As you may recall from the chapter on puppetry skills, a puppeteer must learn to keep a puppet at the correct height and in an upright position. But what happens if the handler's arm gets tired or he or she loses concentration and stops paying attention to the puppet? The puppet starts to sink into the stage or to lean in one direction or the other. That's OK if the sinking or leaning is part of the script. However, if it's because the puppeteer is not paying attention or is feeling tired, then the puppet will no longer be believable as a self-animating character. Instead, the audience will begin to see it for what it is—a lifeless object in the hands of a tired puppeteer.

To keep the puppet at a consistent height, there are two things you can do. The first is to condition your arms so you can keep the puppet upright at all times. The second is to maintain eye contact with the puppet. That way you can monitor the puppet's height and make any necessary adjustments when you find yourself letting the puppet start to sink or lean. If

This elegant marionette appears to be drooping, the result of a tired puppeteer.

the puppet does drop below the level of the stage, just slowly raise it to the proper height. Whatever you do, avoid "popping" it up to the correct position.

It's All in the Swing

Another puppetry peril to avoid, especially when working with rod puppets, is keeping the puppet's arms outstretched and immobile for no apparent reason. In real life, we humans don't walk around with our arms frozen in one position. When we're walking, we normally swing our arms. When we're having a conversation, we use our arms to communicate or emphasize what we're saying with our words. To preserve the lifelike qualities of your puppet, you'll need to practice manipulating its arms in a way that appears natural. The movements should correspond to what the puppet is saying or doing and not be random, unrelated movements.

Here's another tip for moving your puppet's arms in a manner that reinforces its lifelike quality: alternate moving the right and left arm, but not one after the other. People tend to use one arm more than the other, depending on whether they're left- or right-handed. You can imitate this tendency with the way you animate your puppet: use one of its arms more than the other.

The Eyes Have It!

Have you ever looked into a puppet's eyes? If you have, then you know they don't look back at you. (If they do look back, then you may have stumbled upon an extraterrestrial. Just kidding.) The eyes of a puppet are only capable of a blank and lifeless stare—until they are brought to life through the manipulative skills of a puppeteer. According to an old saying, "The eyes are the windows of the soul." Puppets, however, have no souls, no interior life of their own. The only life they have is the one you give them. When performing onstage, it's

This puppeteer clearly understands the importance of maintaining eye contact with his rod puppet.

absolutely essential to make sure not a moment goes by when your puppet is not looking at someone or something. Your puppet's focused, deliberate attention will go a long way toward reinforcing the illusion you are trying to create—that the puppet is alive and responsive to whomever and whatever is in its immediate environment.

To achieve this lifelike effect, when one puppet is talking to another puppet, they need to be looking at each other instead of off to one side, out into the audience, or up into space. However, each puppet should not just be staring at the other puppet the whole time. In real life, two people having a conversation are likely to look away from time to time instead of always keeping their eyes fixed on each other. So having your puppet occasionally look away is OK, so long as the focus soon returns to the other puppet. Some experienced puppeteers recommend turning the puppet's head only part of the way when speaking or listening to another puppet. That way, more of the puppet's face and facial expressions are visible to the audience.

Here's something else to keep in mind regarding a puppet's eye contact, or lack thereof: when the puppet looks directly at the audience, a practical suggestion is to have the puppet's eyes focus on the front row. It may sound illogical, but actually, the rest of the audience will feel the puppet is making eye contact with them even when the puppet's focus is only on the front row. However, having the puppet turn and face the audience should be done sparingly (unless the entire performance is one puppet addressing the audience and not any other puppets or puppeteers).

In most cases, eye contact should be maintained between the puppeteer and his puppet, or between the puppets themselves. When eye contact is lost, it may be because the puppeteer's arm is tired and, as a result, he or she is paying less attention to the puppet and more attention to keeping an arm raised. Or it may be the result of the puppet's position. If you're left-handed and holding a hand puppet on the right side of the stage, you're going to have a difficult time keeping your puppet's eyes focused on a puppet to your left. The same applies to someone who is right-handed and needs the puppet to look to the right.

Speak Out

Puppets come to life not only through their movements and gestures but through the way they speak—their voices. Voice work in puppetry is one more place where problems can arise. If the audience is having trouble hearing and understanding what

TIM'S BIG ADVENTURE WITH PUPPET THEATER

Here's a true story about a young man who thought staging a five-minute puppet show for young children would be a "piece of cake." Tim began by researching available scripts. He didn't like any of them, so he decided to write his own script. Alas, his creativity got the better of him, and he ended up needing five additional puppets to handle a dream sequence in the story. Without a second puppeteer, the play would be impossible to perform, at least the way Tim had written it. Fortunately, his wife agreed to serve as the second puppeteer.

But he still didn't have the extra puppets he needed until he recruited a friend to lend a hand. By now, Tim's imagination was in overdrive: he was convinced the dream sequence really needed clouds of fog. So he bought a fog machine and persuaded his son to handle the fog. The machine worked quite well once it was up and running. The problem was the sound it made the moment the pump kicked in and rolling clouds of steam appeared. It sounded like someone breaking wind.

So Tim purchased a set of clip-on lights with colored lightbulbs to distract the audience when the fog machine was turned on. Of course, the lights would need extension cords and enough electrical outlets. Unfortunately, the place didn't have enough outlets. As a result, Tim and his family did the show before two dozen children with the rude, laugh-producing sound of the fog machine going full blast—and no lights to mask the sound.

a puppeteer is saying, then the performer's **diction** might be the cause. He or she may not be speaking slowly enough and not pronouncing words clearly, speaking too softly, or failing to project his or her voice so people in the last row can hear the words.

A puppeteer using different voices for different puppet characters may fail to make each voice distinctive. Instead, the voices sound too much the same. As a result, the audience won't always be able to tell which character is supposed to be speaking. To correct this problem, the puppeteer needs to practice at home. He or she could invite a friend or family member to watch a rehearsal and then provide feedback about the character voices and whether they're distinguishable. Another possible solution is for the puppeteer to stick with one puppet and one voice until becoming more experienced in using his or her voice to express character.

Tim's Perilous Pitfalls

What can we learn from Tim's big adventure—as described on page 71—in puppet theater? Here's a partial list of "takeaways," or lessons. Which ones do you think are useful and practical ways to avoid making the kinds of mistakes Tim made? Which ones are completely preposterous and not meant to be taken seriously?

1. Never try to write your own script for a puppet play.
2. For a five-minute puppet play, make the story as complicated as you can.

3. If you're a solo puppeteer, operating many puppets in one show will make you a better performer.

4. Know as much about the performance venue as you can before the day of the show.

5. Don't hesitate to use special effects, even if they will interfere with the show.

6. Expect the sponsor of your show to go out of his or her way to give you what you need for the show.

7. Plan your show with a clear understanding of what is or is not available at the performance venue.

Actually, only items 4 and 7 are genuine tips for avoiding some of the problems Tim faced. Tim's first mistake was making the script more complicated than it needed to be for a five-minute show. Also, he added more puppet characters than he had on hand, and with only a few weeks before the day of the show, he had to scramble to make the additional puppets. The dream sequence in his script might have been a nice touch and could have really added to the performance. And the fog machine was also an interesting choice. But he already knew during rehearsals that the machine made some pretty nasty sounds. Still, he used it anyway. A better choice might have been to find some other way to create the dreamlike atmosphere he wanted, perhaps by using evocative music along with imaginative lighting.

You don't need expensive materials for your puppets. This artist is working with foam.

CHAPTER FIVE

Real-World Careers

In this chapter, we'll explore some of the career paths that puppetry can prepare you for in the world outside of theater. Puppetry, like other performing arts, encompasses a broad range of skills that can be applied to careers in education, counseling, communications, and business management, among other fields. But that's not all. With a background in puppetry, you might find your future job niche in a related medium like fashion, television, film, or even live-actor theater. But before we take a look at some of the ways in which puppetry can help you move into a real-world occupation, let's consider the career of someone who went in the opposite direction—from a secure, full-time job to becoming a professional puppeteer.

"Ciao, Baby"

In 2014, Gwen Dean quit her job, and she did it in a very public way. In fact, Gwen's resignation instantly became a big hit on the internet. So what exactly happened? Well, during a Super Bowl ad for the web-hosting business GoDaddy, she announced to millions of viewers, including her boss, Ted, that she was officially leaving her position as a machine engineer. "I quit," she said while operating a cuddly blue puppet. Her last words to her boss were "Ciao, baby," Italian for "good-bye."

She left her well-paid job to pursue her dream career—managing her own puppet business, Puppets by Gwen. She has no regrets about her decision. Her choice of a new career didn't just come out of the blue; she had been doing puppetry on the side for the previous two years. That experience showed her what she really wanted to do with her life, and then she found the courage to do it, even if that meant sacrificing the financial security that came with her work as an engineer. Fortunately, her drastic career move paid off in more ways than one. For starters, Gwen soon found herself booking more puppet shows than she could handle by herself. As her business expanded, she realized she would need to become an employer and hire others to help her. Now she has two employees who actually do the puppet shows and an assistant to organize the bookings. Thanks to her skill, her passion for the art of puppetry, and her keen business expertise, Gwen is enjoying continuing success, with plans to offer puppet-making workshops and to write a book about the engineering that goes into puppetry. Plus, she has her own line of original handmade puppets—by Gwen, of course.

Getting Ready to Launch

So what else can you do with a background in puppetry besides becoming a puppeteer? To answer that question, we need to look carefully at some of the specific skill areas that puppetry can develop and how these skills can be transferred to other types of careers. Let's start with the most obvious: acting. A puppeteer speaks through whatever puppets he or she is animating. The puppeteer has to be able to create different voices for each puppet and to become skilled in basic acting techniques, like developing a character; expressing the character's feelings through voice, movement, and gesture; understanding the elements that make up a script; creating relationships with other characters; and relating to an audience. A career in the theater as a professional actor may be just the right step for someone with experience in puppetry.

Performing onstage is only one among a number of possible options for someone interested in acting. If that's where your interests lie, you might also audition for roles in television shows or movies. The competition is fierce, but you won't know if this path is right for you until you actually put yourself out there and give it your best shot. To prepare for an

Aspiring actors gather to audition for a new Austin Powers movie. The man at left fully dressed for the part.

acting career, you might consider majoring in theater arts. That way, you'll get the training you need to work in many forms of media, each of which requires its own specific skills in addition to fundamental acting skills.

What's Your Major?

Some theater arts programs include courses in puppetry, while some universities offer puppetry majors to their undergraduate students. For example, the University of Connecticut (UConn) was one of the first schools to offer a bachelor of fine arts degree in puppet arts. At one point in its history, the university was the only school that also offered a master of fine arts degree in puppetry. It continues to offer these degree programs to students, many of whom go on to work for theaters around the world as performers and designers. Graduates of the puppet programs also find promising careers in television and film. Others write books, design toys, work as grade school teachers, and develop programs for museums. According to the university's website, puppetry majors have created nearly five hundred puppet shows since 1964, the year when UConn launched its first puppetry courses.

The university views puppetry as an art form that embraces most of the arts as well as the sciences and humanities. As evidence of puppetry's universal appeal, UConn's graduate program in puppet arts has included students with undergraduate degrees in such fields as acting, architecture, costuming, design, English literature, mechanical engineering, and music.

An undergraduate majoring in puppetry can choose among a rich and varied menu of courses. Here are just a few:

- Puppet Performance
- Theater Production
- History of Drama
- Vocal Performance Techniques
- Script Analysis
- Advanced Puppetry Techniques I and II
- Trends in Contemporary American Puppet Theater
- Costume Design
- Lighting Design

Designing Careers

If your experience in puppetry includes designing puppet costumes or puppet stages, or even making your own puppets, then you might pursue a career in some aspect of design. Depending on what sort of design experience and/or training you've had, you could find yourself working in the fashion industry, or designing sets or costumes for movies, TV shows, or plays. If you have experience designing lighting and sound for elaborate puppet productions, then consider applying these design skills in other fields where lighting and sound are necessary. Did you ever

Lighting designers pulled out all the stops to celebrate Jordin Sparks's *American Idol* victory.

watch the TV show *American Idol*? Kieran Healy, the lighting designer for that show, had a field day creating spectacular lighting displays for the openings and for each vocal performance.

The Written Word

Some puppeteers may enjoy writing their own scripts. Writing scripts that will appeal to children is a terrific way to learn how to write other types of child-centered materials, such as books, television scripts, or movie scripts for children. But as you know by now, the art of puppetry isn't just for children. Some of the most successful Broadway plays and musicals have featured human actors and puppets together onstage. *Avenue Q*, *The Lion King*, and *War Horse* are stunning examples of this combination.

Animatronics

In film, puppets as mechanically controlled devices have played many important roles.

Let's go back in time to the year 1982. That's when the movie *E.T. the Extra-Terrestrial* was released. It's a science fiction fantasy about an alien and his relationship with Elliott, a young boy who helps him get back to his own world. In fact, E.T. was a puppet, or more specifically, an animatronic or robotic device. For scenes shot indoors, special sets were designed to accommodate the animatronic version of E.T., since the puppet was so heavy it needed to be bolted to the floor. A team of ten puppeteers watching TV monitors operated mechanical controls that allowed them to perform around 150 different motions.

Besides the animatronic E.T., there were three other versions of the character. They were used in close-ups to show facial expressions or in scenes in which E.T. is shown walking. For these scenes, three different human actors were employed. In addition, a professional mime provided E.T.'s hand movements.

The success of movies like *E.T. the Extra-Terrestrial* illustrates the influence of animatronics in the film industry. Animatronics involves the

CINDY DERBY, FROM PUPPETEER TO AUTHOR

Since childhood, Cindy Derby has been drawn to the visual arts, particularly painting. While studying in Glasgow, Scotland, for her master's degree, she discovered the world of puppetry. People were creating amazing puppet shows that took this art form in new directions. Derby was so inspired by their remarkable creativity that she decided to create her own one-woman puppet show. As a visual artist, she made her own puppets and rehearsed the show inside her very small room in Glasgow. Later on, Derby wrote an original puppet show about a little green man who lives in a tree made of spools. As her reputation grew, she started making larger puppets and performing her shows in larger venues in cities around the world.

Derby's performing experience didn't begin with puppetry. Before becoming a puppeteer, she worked

manipulation of mechanized puppets either by remote control or with the aid of computer programs. Like E.T., the shark in the movie *Jaws* and many of the dinosaurs in *Jurassic Park* were animatronic creatures. In *Jurassic Park III*, the film's production team designed and created Spinosaurus, an animatronic dinosaur so huge it towered over the Tyrannosaurus rex (T-rex) in the original *Jurassic Park*.

To become an animatronics specialist, you'll probably need to combine several different strands in theater as an actor. She's also been a production designer for film, an art teacher, and even a stand-up comedian. While living abroad, she studied with the London School of Puppetry. Her talent was recognized by the Jim Henson Foundation and Puppet Animation Scotland, which awarded her grants so she could develop her puppetry.

Derby's strong visual sense and her love of storytelling eventually led her in a new artistic direction. Although her love of puppets and puppetry is never far behind her, she now devotes her life to writing and illustrating children's books. She loves to tell stories through pictures and creates her illustrations by using mixed media, including watercolors, charcoal pencils, and crayons. Her picture book *How to Walk an Ant* is scheduled to be published by Roaring Brook Press in 2019.

of study. Sally Corporation is a leading animatronics business serving the needs of amusement parks, museums, and other clients. Its robotic figures include zombies, pirates, a giant singing bear, and other large animals. Designers, artists, sculptors, and technicians integrate art and technology to create extremely lifelike robots, or mechanical puppets.

If you have a creative streak and are interested in applying your background in puppetry to the field of animatronics, enrollment in a school that offers

This mechanical creature performed in a stage show called *Walking with Dinosaurs.*

programs in entertainment design may be just the ticket. For example, the Art Institute of Pittsburgh features a bachelor of science in this subject. Students will learn about special effects and how to design animatronic systems. They'll also take courses in architecture and the use of computer technology to create animatronics. The curriculum is designed to enable students to apply their skills to theme parks, historic sites, museums, and similar venues where special effects and robotic devices are needed.

Stop-Motion Animation

The magic of puppetry is seeing inanimate objects come to life thanks to the skills of the puppeteer. Operating a hand puppet or manipulating the strings of a marionette, for example, are traditional animation methods. Using electronic tools to control the movements of robotic devices like E.T. or a T-rex is a modern form of animation using the latest technology. So is stop-motion animation, not to be confused with animatronics. Stop-motion **animators** work with an inanimate object (or character), one photographic frame at a time. For each successive frame, the object is moved slightly by the animator. When the frames are run rapidly together, the object appears to be moving. In other words, it comes to life.

The characters in your favorite video games are created by animators. So are many of the characters in TV commercials, cartoons, and movies. TV ads bring many engaging characters to life, such as M&Ms, the GEICO Gecko, and Crayola characters Denny, Scarlet, Gus, and Rod. But entertainment isn't

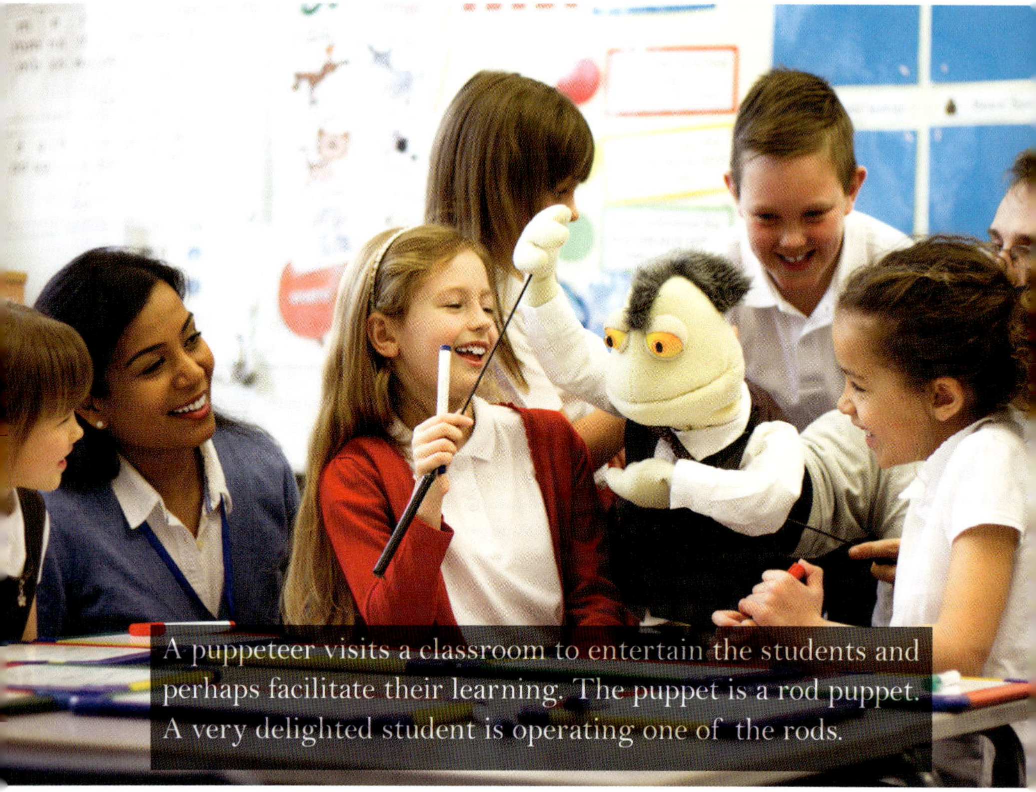

A puppeteer visits a classroom to entertain the students and perhaps facilitate their learning. The puppet is a rod puppet. A very delighted student is operating one of the rods.

the only area in which animation plays an important role. As a global industry, animation is used in education, architecture, medicine, advertising, and other fields.

Teaching and Counseling

If the world of high-tech animation doesn't appeal to you, a background in puppetry could be just the thing for a career in education or counseling. In fact, both teachers and therapists may find occasions in which the use of puppets will further their goals, whether educational or therapeutic. In therapeutic situations, the therapist can invite a client to select a puppet, which then becomes an independent character. Instead of the client telling the therapist directly what he or she is feeling or experiencing, the client can charge the puppet with the task of speaking on his or her behalf. A skilled therapist will then interview the puppet, and in the process, both client and therapist will come closer to the truth of just what is going on in the client's life.

In the classroom, children who have a hard time expressing themselves may benefit from holding and operating simple hand puppets, and using the puppets to say what's on their mind, ask or answer questions, or share their feelings. And putting on a puppet show is an activity that will involve the entire class in an activity requiring teamwork and cooperation while developing each child's self-confidence. Plus, puppetry in the classroom can be a great way to enrich the social studies or language arts curriculums, for instance, and to integrate a variety of art forms, like creative writing, visual arts, and dramatic arts.

GLOSSARY

animate To make something move and appear alive.

animator An artist who creates images that appear to come to life on screen. Their work is found in feature films, commercials, computer games, and other media.

animatronics The technique of making and operating lifelike robots, typically for use in movies or other entertainment.

blocking The director's work of positioning actors and puppets onstage and setting their entrances, exits, and other movement.

Bunraku A form of Japanese puppet theater in which puppeteers, dressed in black and visible to the audience, manipulate large puppets to the accompaniment of a chanted narration and musical instruments.

constructed actor Another term for "puppet," since the actor has been constructed from various materials.

control board A device with bars at right angles to a central bar that animates a marionette through the use of wires or strings connecting the bars to body parts such as the hands, shoulders, back, and head.

diction The quality of vocal expression. If a puppeteer is speaking for the puppet, he or she needs to have good diction so the audience can understand what is said.

dolly A platform on wheels or a roller used to move heavy objects.

ensemble A group of people. In the context of this book, it refers to the group of people who are participating in putting on a performance with puppets.

execute To perform or do a job or function as designed.

genre A type or category of play or other work of art.

marionette A puppet moved (animated) through the use of a control board that has strings or wires connected to the knees, wrists, and other body parts.

mitten head A type of hand puppet in which the puppeteer uses his or her thumb to manipulate the character's lower jaw, while the other four fingers control the expressions of the face.

off book Actors who have memorized their lines are said to be "off book" because they no longer need to look at the script.

pantin A two-dimensional cutout of a human character with a jointed body and limbs. Pulling a single cord makes both the arms and legs move up.

preview An advance showing of a performance.

project When used as a verb, it refers to speaking loudly enough, without shouting, so that everyone in the audience can hear you.

puppeteer Someone who works with puppets.

puppet wrangler A person who manages the puppets backstage and is responsible for keeping them in working order and with proper costumes.

repertoire A collection or set of shows that a company or person is ready to perform.

rod puppet A puppet operated and supported by a rod or rods. It usually has a central, vertical rod attached to the head, and a shorter rod attached to each hand.

strike When part or all of the puppets, any sets, plus temporary lighting instruments and sound equipment are removed at the end of a scene or a run.

synchronization The operation or activity of two or more things at the same time. A ventriloquist must throw his or her voice at the same time as the puppet's mouth moves so they are "in sync."

ventriloquist A person skilled in speaking so that his or her voice seems to come from a puppet (or another source).

venue A place where a performance is held.

verisimilitude The appearance of being true or real.

FOR MORE INFORMATION

Books

Blumenthal, Eileen. *Puppetry: A World History.* New York: Abrams, 2005.

Currell, David. *Making and Manipulating Marionettes.* Wiltshire, UK: Crowood Press, 2004.

Lambeth, Cheralyn. *The Well-Dressed Puppet: A Guide to Creating Puppet Costumes.* Burlington, MA: Focal Press, 2015.

Stadelman, Paul, and Bruce Fife. *Ventriloquism Made Easy: How to Talk to Your Hand Without Looking Stupid!* Colorado Springs, CO: Piccadilly Books, 2003.

Videos

Bunraku Theater
https://www.youtube.com/watch?v=f4G68civvo8
Japan's public broadcasting network provides a segment on this ancient art form, demonstrating the teamwork described in chapter 2.

Disney Presents *The Lion King*
https://www.youtube.com/watch?v=27ucbJq510A
Watch how animals are brought to life in a performance of the "Circle of Life" by the Tony Award-winning cast.

The Genius Puppetry Behind *War Horse*: Handspring Puppet Company
https://www.youtube.com/watch?v=h7u6N-cSWtY
Beginning with the tale of a hyena's supple paw, puppeteers Adrian Kohler and Basil Jones tell the story of their latest astonishment: the wonderfully lifelike Joey, the War Horse, who trots (and gallops) convincingly onto the TED Talks stage. Mentioned in chapter 1.

How to Make a Puppet!
https://www.youtube.com/watch?v=NY34Kb5h34s
This video describes how to make a hand puppet out of foam.

The Muppet Show
https://www.youtube.com/watch?v=IvnHgKkNKR4
This video is from the first season and has been watched by nearly a million people.

Puppet Wrangling Backstage at *Avenue Q*
https://www.youtube.com/watch?v=Zq93Umabm9Y
This is a fun time-lapse recording (in necessary low light) of the puppet wrangler responsible for all offstage handling of puppets, including the changing of costumes, for *Avenue Q*.

Vermont's Bread and Puppet Theater—WildTravelsTV.com
https://www.youtube.com/watch?v=OV232D962pE
The Bread and Puppet Theater of Glover, Vermont, has been putting on shows since the 1960s, with puppets that can be more than 20 feet (6 m) tall.

Websites

PuppetBuilder
http://www.puppetbuilder.com
Nick Barone, a professional puppeteer, provides free information on how to make your own puppets, as well as other resources.

Puppeteers of America
https://www.puppeteers.org
This national nonprofit organization has produced hundreds of national and regional festivals to celebrate and share the art of puppetry. Its website lists theaters, resources for professional development, and much more.

Sandglass Theater
http://sandglasstheater.org
This company, mentioned in chapter 3, is breaking new ground in puppetry. Check out the Resources and Workshops tabs, as well as On Tour for its New England touring schedule.

INDEX

Page numbers in **boldface** are illustrations. Entries in boldface are glossary terms.

ABOUT THE AUTHOR

When **George Capaccio** was a child, he loved watching TV shows featuring puppets. His favorite shows were *The Howdy Doody Show* and *Kukla, Fran and Ollie.* As a young man, George worked in children's theater as a performer, director, and scriptwriter. This experience inspired him to become a professional storyteller. His performing skill eventually landed him a job as the host of a children's television show. George is still telling stories, but nowadays, he's also writing them—for all ages.